BOXES WITH
ZERO TOLERANCE

BOXES WITH ZERO TOLERANCE

Poems by
Emmy Pérez

Mouthfeel Press is an indie press. We publish poetry, fiction, and nonfiction in English and Spanish by new and established poets and writers.

Cover Design: Enzo Rodríquez Suárez
Interior Design: Kimberly James
Cover art: Octavio Quintanilla, 74 Equilibrium, "Tendedero in Moonlight"
Contact Information: info.mouthfeelbooks@gmail.com

ISBN: 978-1-957840-48-2

Published in the United States, 2025

First Printing in English
$12

MOUTHFEEL PRESS

CONTENTS

*To all who carry protest signs in the streets or in their hearts
and feel like their empathy is not enough.
And to those whose empathy is stirring again.*

Boxes with Zero Tolerance

1.

I said I'd never write a sonnet. Because
I don't like counting syllables on my
fingers like tapping up what I failed

to internalize. And forget about
iambic pentameter like so many
colonies ago. I can barely listen to

my once-beloved *before you go-go* radio
anymore. And the quest for "perfection"

stymies like a sty caught in periphery—
our elders warning, *Don't watch a dog crap!*

And yet, here I draw a little box
for delivery, not coffin, nor Kleenex,
because I love you and don't want to die.

2.

Because I love you and don't want to die,
my body plays persuasion by oxytocin.
Maybe we can still make more babies.
I'm still bleeding away and many still
rock like fertility folks in basalt
and sculpted in clay. Pleasure more ancient

than maíz. Sometimes joy takes decades
questioning teenage forevers. Maybe

we agree, love, with all due respect, our
unwavering forevers are the little ones
and some elders, bonds that surpass romance-
flowed-oaths, tested and paperish as this.

And yet, the eternal isn't blood, flowers,
or gender: this urge to familial love.

3.

This urge for familial love flowers
geographies past, present, future/forever,
beyond twin cities and bi-river flows thru
earth-beds, beyond canals and dams that thwart
new resacas for insatiable capital and control.

I am from abuela/os who migrated
from Guanajuato, from Chihuahua,
and an abuelo from cottonwoods this side
of el río. My mom, my dad, born here,

and our concentric circles map like a liver
in México and a heart not stopped by river
cops. These organs, not papeles, persist

on unceded land and "ceded" after white
flags, pennied treaties, even one in millions.

In 1930, my tatarabuela still spoke Rarámuri.

4.

In 1930, my tatarabuela
still spoke Rarámuri.   Sometimes the census

affirms so-called myths and has erased,
erases much more like the church, like empire

when it finds voice in us—on Turtle Island,
Abya Yala, in all languages and directions

of the elements. Brown people still marked "white"
some say   equally   as if   a desired

shortcut   consolation   consensus.   We

chant *Say Her Name: ¡Claudia Patricia Gómez González!*
and remember Sandra Bland—may she rest in love

and power forever—never made it to her alma mater

interview. Say it with me if you agree:
I don't choose whiteness to grant me more rights

even when whiteness lets me pass or doesn't
choose me. Intergenerational

trauma half-lives (half-līves). We survive
and thrive and sometimes the tactics scar.

If they built their wall near you, you'd think
music left for rhetoric too.

5.

You'd think music left for rhetoric too.
Children snatched from families, locked up
in separate states or cities without
a tracking system in place. *Will this happen*

to us? my four-year-old asks, six-year-old
listening. No, we're not seeking asylum.
Let's go with LUPE. Make signs. Protest

La Hielera: *¡Niños, no están solos!*

¡Niñas, no están solas!   *¡Gobierno*

mentiroso—el pueblo está furioso!

¡El pueblo unido jamás será vencido!

When a bus leaves Ursula, Central Processing
Center, children's faces fog bus windows—
their parents told their children are bathing.

6.

"They are the ones who broke the law, they are the ones who endangered their own children on their trek. The United States on the other hand, goes to extraordinary lengths to protect them while the parents go through a short detention period." —Jeff Sessions

They are the ones who were told their children
were taken to bathe—and not returned. They

are the ones whose nursing babies and toddlers
were forced to wean and left in wet diapers.

And their other young ones also cried
for mami, for papá, for tía, for _____

and were told they were an *orchestra without
a conductor.* And enough in this country

elected the conductor with his fist
in the air, without music, without ocean,

without moon, without the very earth. He
was the one and she another and he yet

another who said they'd be taking her child
the next day and proclaimed *Happy Mother's Day.*

7.

The next day too he'd said *Feliz día
de las madres.* Rain and thunder pound

McAllen. Jobs are jobs, implied—too kind.
Parents or not. Once immigrants or not.

Cops are cops. Thunder. The streets flood all night.
My kids wake and cuddle near, cannot sleep,

and all I can think is la hielera,
the so-called and dreaded perrera, eight

miles from here, and more further away, all
the children inside. Officers' cruel lies—

don't tell me this shows heart: *Your dad's going
to come later on another plane.* Their vents

to parents: *When will you stop coming? Better
if a bomb were set off in your countries.*

8.

Officer rants, *Better if a bomb were set . . .*
Sessions admonishes even his *church
friends,* ignores humanitarians, here

and far who deliver food, clean water,
clothes for all bridge-sides. Metered asylum

seekers wait and wait. Here, released adults leave
clamped with ankle monitors, welcomed at respite
centers offering meals, toothbrushes, showers.
Bus transfers explained and Sharpied on envelopes.

Obey the laws, he warns, *because God
has ordained them for the purpose of order.*

McAllen protest sign: *God has Ordained ICE
for Raspas.* Sabores de arco iris. Stop pawning

children to build more empire—cha-ching.

9.

Children jailed in empire's walls—cha-ching.

Earth, I used to spend time loving you—I
stared at your bees, listened to your nighthawks
I hear again while marching Brownsville streets
to Casa El Presidente prison for babies
and other tender-aged children. Anacahuita
star-bells and zancudos follow vigil signs
and gospel songs as organizers shout
Shame on you! to brown men parading
out the facility in a posse.

A woman camped there with her son sings
Tracy Chapman's *talkin' bout a revolution*

over a week after FLOTUS flew with fashion-
mouth: *I REALLY DON'T CARE, DO U?*

10.

FLOTUS wore *I REALLY DON'T CARE, DO U?*
on the plane and back, over a week ago,

day after an executive order to pause
its own abuse, thousands taken, lost.

Tonight, the tender age facility posse
care, don't care, care, don't—of course
they're pissed, we're on their border now,
can't cross the lot like mosquitos. We're

lighting candles, singing because song is
movement. Someday you'll know many felt powerless
and still tried. Someday you'll tell stories of your lives.

These boxes crave sun, a splash of rain, Gulf
dunes with morning glories opening. And shore
packed taut by warm waves, sea turtle hatchlings.

11.

Turtle hatchlings reached the Gulf's warm waters

while the posse of men marched out the facility
like the enlisted. One revved a big truck
in the parking lot, skidded like making himself
appear bigger to a bear. And the staff
inside feeding and changing children remained

faceless to us. Did they help the babies sleep
or let them cry it out? Did they gain trust
with the grieving and any of the bereaved?
What else could some know? Shift jefes shout

chain of command. DC adviser-bigots plotted
policy and pleased the man. DHS boss behind
a mic like this mic, but on tv with bombshell
blonde hair and as the whole country listened.

"Los niños lloran, no reconocen nuestras voces, y se sienten abandonados y sin amor. Esto nos hace sentir muertos en vida"

–group letter by detained mothers,
Port Isabel Service Detention Center

12.

She stood and spoke as the whole country listened.
Bragged all her staff are bilingual, paperwork

in English and Spanish. A six-year-old
on the phone speaking his native Q'eqchi':

*Papá, I thought they killed you. You separated
from me. You don't love me anymore?*

                    If this crushes you too,
maybe you'd understand wanting
to compose beautiful songs without words

for children of war, children caught in any crossfire.

But part of my truth is I delete. Eek. How naive
to think we'd reach the audience, much less
with what they most need, and literary

Twitter would diss the audacity. Even all this
too.   And I betray my body which once
gave light and instead restrain spilled rants
in English for adults like me as that staff

commands: *Sign this and that form* in English
or Spanish—signatures more "legal" than

people. English is a lie. Spanish is
not enough. Silence is a lie. And asylum.

13.

English is a lie. Silence, a lie. And asylum.

They *seem* safer for now reunited
with caldo and pan dulce. The father
reports his son has been returned to him
ill—as in no nation's pills can heal.

I'd too trust the reporter and public
more than an ICE-y ankle monitor too tight.

I've never wanted to become a lawyer
or learn hierbas like a curandera

until now. I've never yearned for more money
than I need and triple the time: donate
to Angry Tías and Abuelas RGV,
TCRP, LUPE, and other loving orgs

as 45's minions continue to king him.

14.

One man and his minions cannot take all.

You know the quetzal cannot be caged,
said a detained teen, of a collective image
teens drew in Tornillo, *because otherwise*
it will die of sadness.   Glyphs
pop green, red, yellow, turquoise, orange, blue,
brown. Mayans have studied the sky and time

much longer than 1492.   We'll vote him
and his tweet laws out, a great fall
from his highest walls. Survivors will grow,
testify and publish, justice in their art and lives.

We wish them healing outdoors and fresh food,
safety, family, community that speaks
their mother tongues, wisdoms. Continued love

15.

I said I'd never write a sonnet. Because
I love you and don't want to die.
This urge for familial love flowers.
In 1930, my tatarabuela still spoke Rarámuri.

You'd think music left for rhetoric too.
They are the ones told their children are bathing.
Feliz día de las madres he snides
and another rants: *Better if a bomb were set* . . .

Children stolen, double walled in—cha-ching.
She wore *I REALLY DON'T CARE, DO U?*

Turtle hatchlings reach the Gulf's warm waters
as he stands and brags while the country cringes.
English is a lie. Silence is a lie. And asylum.

The dethroned man will try to crown himself again.

Postscript Newsreel

The dethroned man will try to crown himself
again even when voted out. His minutemen

staged an insurrection at the Capitol
for him on Día de los Tres Reyes

Magos. Three years later, a billionaire
donated hundreds of millions in campaign

funds to help king the-now-convicted-felon
as oligarchic rockets colonize

and pollute the Río Grande Delta,
the Gulf of Mexico and more. The platform:

deport deport deport. ICE abducts in daylight.
Mothers scream *¡Auxilio! ¡Mis hijos!*

¡Suéltenme! ¡Mis hijos están en la escuela!

Notes

"It just happened that in 2018 we had cell phones and social media to report on it in real time almost, but our history is replete of instances where immigrants who were not considered white have been treated terribly by government"
—Efrén C. Olivares

Olivares [author of *My Boy Will Die of Sorrow*] quote as transcribed from "Ep 42: Resilience, Storytelling and Justice: Efrén Olivares on Immigration and Family Separation." Power Up Your Practice podcast, YouTube. Nov. 25, 2024.

#1. Partial song title quoted from Wham's 1984 album *Make It Big*

#2. Thanks to jo reyes-boitel for a suggestion in another context

#4. "Say Her Name": Poets Against Walls Collective performance at the Vigil for Claudia Patricia Gomez Gonzalez at Basilica of Our Lady San Juan Del Valle, June 28, 2018. Hosted by RGV No Border Wall Movement, La Union Del Pueblo Entero (LUPE), Carrizo/Comecrudo Tribe of Texas, Border Workers United, and Lower Rio Grande Valley Sierra Club.

#5. Chants quoted were led by LUPE and Centro de Trabajadores Fuerza del Valle. Father's Day Vigil Ursula Detention Center protest, June 17, 2018, McAllen, TX, hosted by Border Workers United, LUPE, National Domestic Workers Alliance, United We Dream, ACLU, America's Voice, People's Action, Women's Refugee Commission, and Faith in Action / #FamiliesBelongTogether.

#6 & #8. "The are the ones" and "church friends" (and other quotes) by the Attorney General: "Sessions cites Bible to defend immigration policies resulting in family separations," by Tal Kopan. *CNN* online. June 14, 2018.

#6. "The baritone voice of a Border Patrol agent booms [in Spanish] above the crying. 'Well, we have an orchestra here,' he jokes. 'What's missing is a conductor.' From "Listen To The Children Who've Just Been Separated From Their Parents At The Border" by Ginger Thompson. *ProPublica* online, June 18, 2018.

#6. Angelica Gonzalez-Garcia: "The day after I was detained, I was removed from the cell and … told that they were going to take my daughter a long way away" and "One of the officers asked me, 'In Guatemala, do they celebrate Mother's Day?' When I answered yes, he said, 'Then Happy Mother's Day,' because the next Sunday was Mother's Day. I lowered my head so that my daughter would not see tears forming in my eyes" from "ICE agent told immigrant mom 'Happy Mother's Day' then took her daughter away, lawsuit says." *CNN* online. June 30, 2018.

#7. "Your dad is going to come later on a plane" M. Guidos from *Separated: Children at the Border*, documentary, *Frontline PBS* online, 2020.

#7. "When we arrived to the United States on May 18, the officers said… when would we stop coming? [and] that it would be better if a bomb were set off in our countries…." Testimony of Yolani Karina Padilla-Orellana as transcribed in "ICE Agents to Asylum Seekers 'Don't You Know That We Hate You People?: New court documents reveal the cruelty of Trump's family separations" by Tim Dickinson, *Rolling Stone* online. July 10, 2018.

#9. June 30, 2018: Candlelight vigil march at Casa El Presidente in Brownsville (originally scheduled for Casa Padre).

#9. Song title/lyric quote from Tracy Chapman's self-titled album, 1988.

#9 and #10. She "boarded her plane wearing an olive green coat that read, in white capital letters, 'I really don't care. Do U?' [She] did not wear it while visiting with the children, but she did wear it upon her return to the capital" from "Melania Trump Wore a Jacket Saying 'I Really Don't Care' on Her Way to Texas Shelters" by Katie Rogers. *New York Times* online, June 21, 2018.

#11 and #12. DHS Secretary: "this administration did not create a policy of separating families at the border"; "Additionally, all U.S. Border Patrol personnel in the southwest border are bilingual — every last one of them"; "They are directed to clearly explain the relevant process to apprehended individuals, and provide detainees with written documentation in both Spanish and English that lays out the process and appropriate phone numbers to contact" from "Kirstjen Nielsen's mighty struggle tries to explain separating families at the border," by Aaron Blake. *Washington Post* online, June 19, 2018.

#11. "Stephen Miller… [and] Gene Hamilton, a close colleague of Miller's … were pushing for really harsh enforcement policies, including the separation of families. But one of the most interesting things I took away from this story [in *The Atlantic*] was the degree to which people from within the bureaucracy … people who held political roles who had served under Presidents, both Republican and Democrat, also went along with zero tolerance…" and "… I discovered this idea [zero tolerance policy] came from a man named Tom Homan. He was the head of ICE under the Trump administration" –Caitlin Dickerson, in an interview with Geoff Bennett: "How a Trump-era policy that separated thousands of migrant families came to pass." PBS News online, Aug. 13, 2022.

"Los niños lloran, no reconocen nuestras voces, y se sienten abandonados y sin amor. Esto nos hace sentir muertos en vida" –group letter by detained mothers, Port Isabel Service Detention Center in Los Fresnos, TX as transcribed from letter image in "Parents waiting to be reunited with their children write heartbreaking letter" by Rosa Flores, Nick Valencia and Susannah Cullinane, *CNN* online, July 16, 2018.

#12 & #13. Quote "Papá, I thought they…" by Hermelindo Che Coc recalling what his son told him. Also, a paraphrase from "'This is not how I gave them my son,' he said, crying. 'My son has come back to me sick.'" From "'I'm here. I'm here.' Father reunited with son amid tears, relief and fear of what's next," by Esmeralda Bermudez and Marcus Yam, *LA Times* online, July 15, 2018.

#14. "A boy who led the [group drawing] effort told the teacher 'You know the quetzal can't be caged, because it will die of sadness.'" Also, historian Dr. Yolanda Chávez Leyva on co-curating the Uncaged Art exhibit as co-founder of Museo Urbano: "Everything we read was about trauma and suffering. I wanted people to see what was inside of the children, which to me was a lot of creativity and beauty" from "Uncaged Art: The visions of migrant youth from Tornillo" by Kimi Eisele on *BorderLore* blog, Dec. 4, 2019.

#14. Co-founder of Museo Urbano, historian Dr. David Dorado Romo, wrote "Uncaged Art: Finding Life and Light in Art from Detention," in *The Texas Observer* online, April 22, 2019. The article draws attention to the vibrant colors in the artwork and states how "In Guatemala the quetzal is a symbol of hope and freedom." Also "about 6,200 children were confined at Tornillo during the seven-month period it was open." Many were unaccompanied minors and some were separated from their families at the border.

#14. For a first-hand account/memoir of a teen's life and journey to the U.S. (from Honduras) with detainment in Tornillo in 2018, please see: *Detained: A Boy's Journal of Survival and Resilience*, by D. Esperanza and Gerardo Iván Morales, Atria/Primero Sueño Press, 2025.

Postscript quotes from "'Por favor, mis hijos están en la escuela': Mujer suplica a ICE que la dejen ir." Univision San Antonio, YouTube video, May 28, 2025.

Acknowledgments

Grateful acknowledgement to the editors of *The Quarry: A Social Justice Poetry Database*, *Reed Magazine*, and *The Long Devotion: Poets Writing Motherhood* for selecting some of the individual sections, in earlier versions, from this sequence, for publication. *The Long Devotion* anthology also includes an essay that documents the drafting of this work during the height of family separation policies and actions in the summer of 2018. Thank you to Gemini Ink's summer conference 2018, Veronica Golos, Emily (near tocaya) Pérez, Sasha West, Rosebud Ben-Oni, Sarah Dalton-Erickson, Split this Rock, and my RGV family for encouraging this work into fruition in some way. Mil gracias—Maria Miranda Maloney and the Mouthfeel Press team—for publishing this chapbook and to United States Artists and selection committee for the faith in my work at a time I most needed it.

This work is made more possible because of poets/writers, musicians, historians, and/or activists such as Nancy Lorenza Green (QEPD), Yolanda Chávez Leyva, and David Romo, and other incredible people from El Paso to El Valle and beyond, including Efrén Olivares with Texas Civil Rights Project (TCRP) at the time, and Nayelly Barrios with Angry Tías and Abuelas RGV, Tania Chávez and many more organizers at La Union Del Pueblo Entero (LUPE), the Carrizo/Comecrudo Nation, RGV No Border Wall Movement, and fellow Poets Against Walls collective members César L. de León, Celina Gomez, Carolina Monsiváis, and many more folks, too many to name in this space, who uplift others through their time and dedication.